The 7 Keys to AI: Navigating the AI Revolution

All About Artificial Intelligence, Chatbots, Prompts, and Job Applications, Volume 1

J. L .Gallegos

Published by Frank Sagan Media

While every precaution has been taken in the preparation of this book, the publisher assumes no responsibility for errors or omissions, or for damages resulting from the use of the information contained herein.

THE 7 KEYS TO AI: NAVIGATING THE AI REVOLUTION

Written by J. L .Gallegos.

Table of Contents

Chapter 1

AI Unbound: Navigating the Fire of Innovation, Echoing the Spirit of Prometheus.

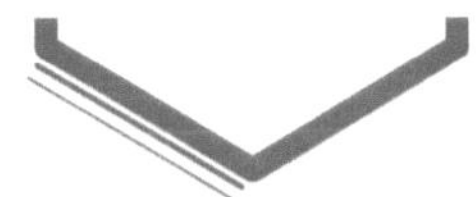

Prometheus was a Titan who took it upon himself to empower humanity with the gift of fire, a divine secret held by the gods. Fire represented not only warmth and light but also the ability to cook food and forge tools—an essential advancement for human civilization.

By stealing fire from the gods and sharing it with humans, Prometheus played a pivotal role in shaping the destiny of humanity. This act of defiance against the gods earned him their wrath. Zeus, the king of the Olympian gods, sought to punish Prometheus for challenging divine authority and upsetting the natural order. As a consequence, Prometheus was subjected to a tormenting punishment: he was bound to a rock, where an eagle would perpetually feast on his liver, only for it to regenerate each night, causing unending agony.

Prometheus' story has been interpreted as a parable of the tension between human progress and divine authority, with Prometheus representing human innovation and the gods symbolizing traditional powers. His gift of fire not only brought enlightenment but also the responsibility of wielding newfound power responsibly.

AI possesses dual potential—it can offer tremendous benefits while also carrying significant risks. It's comparable to Prometheus' gift of fire to humanity, providing the means to shape our world yet demanding responsibility in its usage. The same AI that aids in medical diagnosis can also perpetuate biases, inadvertently embedding societal prejudices into its algorithms.

AI's potential is analogous to Prometheus' fire in another way. It ignites our curiosity, propelling us forward, urging us to envision a future teeming with possibilities. Can AI craft poetry rivaling Shakespeare's? Can it forecast weather patterns to mitigate natural disasters? Can it shape a more promising future for humanity? The answer lies not merely in AI's capabilities, but in our choices, ambitions, and dreams.

The Dartmouth Spark: A Mid-20th Century Workshop Ignites the AI Revolution

The AI landscape had its equivalent of the steam engine during the mid-20th century. In 1956, the Dartmouth Workshop, organized by John McCarthy, Marvin Minsky, Nathaniel Rochester, and Claude Shannon, marked the inception of AI as an academic discipline. Just as the steam engine transformed transportation, this workshop ignited the AI revolution, establishing AI research as a legitimate field of study.

In 1956, the Dartmouth Workshop set the stage for the development of AI, with pioneers like Allen Newell and Herbert A. Simon making the first significant AI program. They created the Logic Theorist, which could prove mathematical theorems and represented the dawn of AI as a research field.

THE AI COMMUNITY FACED its winter, analogous to a period of harsh environmental conditions for a plant. The AI Winter, which lasted through the late '70s and '80s, was marked by overpromising and underdelivering on the capabilities of AI systems. Despite initial enthusiasm, funding and interest waned as early AI projects struggled to meet their lofty goals.

During the AI Winter, Symbolics and LISP Machines, companies that built AI hardware, faced financial difficulties as the AI industry contracted. Their story represents the challenges and financial setbacks that characterized this era.

THE LATE 20TH CENTURY witnessed the resurgence of AI, symbolized by the rebirth of machine learning. Innovations like neural networks and deep learning became the backbone of modern AI. The metaphor of a phoenix rising from the ashes encapsulates this revival, as AI rekindled its potential.

In the 1990s, Yann LeCun's work on Convolutional Neural Networks (CNNs) revolutionized computer vision. Fast forward to the 2010s, and CNNs powered self-driving cars and facial recognition technology, exemplifying the resurgence of AI through machine learning.

AI in Everyday Life: The Fabric of Our Digital Existence

In recent years, AI has become deeply ingrained in our daily lives, similar to how a thread is woven into the fabric of a garment. Virtual assistants like Siri and Alexa, recommendation algorithms on platforms like Netflix, and autonomous vehicles are all examples of AI's omnipresence.

AI-driven recommendation systems on platforms like Amazon or Netflix predict what products or content you might like. They learn from your past choices, creating a personalized experience and shaping how we interact with technology.

THE HISTORICAL EVOLUTION of AI is not a closed chapter but an open canvas, waiting for future innovations and breakthroughs. Just as a painter approaches a blank canvas with boundless creativity, AI's potential remains limitless. Quantum computing, ethical considerations, and the quest for AGI (Artificial General Intelligence) are the exciting frontiers of AI that await exploration.

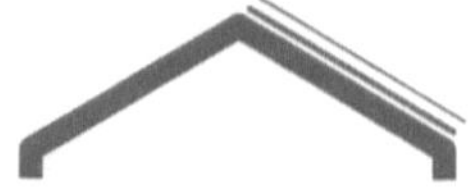

AI: Sleek robots and sci-fi fantasies?

Let us dispel the notion that AI resides solely within the confines of sleek robots and sci-fi fantasies. In truth, AI dwells among us in subtler forms: in recommendation systems that foresee our preferences, in the algorithms that guide our online searches, and even in the spellbinding artistry of self-driving cars navigating through bustling streets. These manifestations are the harmonious notes of AI's symphony, resonating through various facets of our lives.

AI encompasses a spectrum that ranges from narrow to general intelligence. It triumphs in specific tasks, such as classifying images or translating languages. But the latter—the elusive general intelligence—remains the holy grail, aspiring to mimic the holistic reasoning and adaptability of the human mind.

But like a double-edged sword, AI's capabilities and implications evoke profound questions. The unyielding pursuit of progress necessitates caution. As we bestow AI with ever-increasing autonomy, ethical considerations arise like beacons in the night sky. What becomes of our moral compass when AI can discern faces and emotions, raising questions about privacy and surveillance? These reflections underscore the weight of our choices.

So, as we stand at the cusp of AI's evolution, let us not just marvel at the enigma we've unveiled but embrace the challenge of shaping its trajectory. As navigators once relied on stars to guide their way, let us turn to scientific literacy as our guiding star to navigate the complexities of AI and its implications. Let's learn not only to adapt but to flourish in the face of the future.

The roots of AI extend deep into the soil of history, drawing nourishment from the nutrients of mathematical logic, philosophical contemplation, and the raw power of computing. Envision the progression of AI as a river, meandering through time, accumulating the knowledge of ancient civilizations, the wisdom of scholars, and the innovation of modern technologists. Each bend in the river signifies a breakthrough, a leap in understanding, much like a cascade of waterfalls culminating in the birth of neural networks and deep learning algorithms.

However, much like a powerful tool, AI possesses dual potential—it can offer tremendous benefits while also carrying significant risks. It's comparable to Prometheus' gift of fire to humanity, providing the means to shape our world yet demanding responsibility in its usage. The same AI that aids in medical diagnosis can also perpetuate biases, inadvertently embedding societal prejudices into its algorithms.

In the realm of AI, we are akin to astronomers gazing into the cosmos, uncovering new stars and galaxies of possibilities. Yet, like celestial bodies that cast shadows, AI can cast its ethical, social, and economic shadows upon our society. As we unlock AI's secrets, we must ensure we also unlock the ethical compass that guides its actions.

Chapter 2

Artificial intelligence (AI) can be categorized into several types based on its capabilities and applications. Here are some of the main types of AI:

The AI Spectrum: From Narrow to General Intelligence

Narrow or Weak AI (ANI): Narrow AI is designed for a specific task or a narrow range of tasks. It operates within predefined boundaries and doesn't possess general intelligence or awareness.

Narrow AI is like a talented musician who excels in playing a specific instrument, say, the violin. This musician can produce beautiful music, but their expertise is limited to that one instrument. Think of virtual personal assistants like Siri or Alexa. They can answer questions, set reminders, and play your favorite songs, but they don't possess general intelligence.

General or Strong AI (AGI): General AI refers to machines that have human-like intelligence and can perform any intellectual task that a human can. AGI

AGI is the pot of gold at the end of the rainbow, representing machines with human-like intelligence. Usung a metaphor, AGI is like an all-rounder renaissance person who can paint a masterpiece, compose a symphony, and conduct scientific research—all with equal skill. Yet, it is still largely theoretical and has not been achieved. AGI remains a dream on the horizon, as we've not yet created a machine that truly possesses human-like awareness and adaptability.

MACHINE LEARNING (ML): Machine learning is a subset of AI that focuses on the development of algorithms and statistical models that enable computers to improve their performance on a specific task through learning from data.

ML is a vibrant, ever-changing thread that draws from countless data points to make predictions and decisions. Imagine it as a chameleon, adapting its colors to match its environment. A classic example is recommendation systems like Netflix, which use ML to suggest movies based on your viewing history.

Deep Learning: Deep learning is a subset of machine learning that uses artificial neural networks to model and solve complex tasks. It has been particularly successful in image and speech recognition. Deep Learning is a thread as deep and mysterious as the ocean, where neural networks dive into complex tasks. It's like a child learning to recognize animals by looking at pictures in a book. The child may not understand what a "giraffe" is initially, but after seeing many pictures, they become experts at identifying one.

Reinforcement Learning (RL): RL is a type of machine learning where an agent learns how to make sequences of decisions to maximize a reward. It's used in applications like game playing and autonomous robotics.

RL takes you into the world of rewards and punishments, much like training a dog. You offer treats (rewards) for desirable behavior and scold (punishments) for undesirable actions. The dog learns to perform tricks and tasks to maximize treats, similar to how RL works in teaching AI systems to make sequences of decisions.

Natural Language Processing (NLP): NLP is a field of AI that focuses on the interaction between computers and human language. Imagine a bilingual interpreter who effortlessly translates conversations between two people speaking different languages. NLP allows machines to understand and respond in human languages, making chatbots, language translation, and sentiment analysis possible.

Seeing the World Through Machines' Eyes - Computer Vision:

Computer vision involves teaching machines to interpret and understand the visual world.

Computer Vision is like giving machines the gift of sight. It allows them to recognize objects, faces, and scenes in images and videos. It's used in applications like facial recognition and object detection. Think of it as the eyes of autonomous vehicles, enabling them to navigate safely by identifying road signs and pedestrians.

Becoming Experts and Gurus - Expert Systems:

Expert systems are AI programs designed to mimic the decision-making abilities of a human expert in a specific domain, whether in medicine, finance, or law. They use knowledge representation and inference rules to solve problems. Expert Systems are specialized threads that serve as digital advisors in specific domains. Imagine a wise old sage who has spent a lifetime studying a single subject.

Fuzzy Logic: Fuzzy logic is a type of AI that deals with reasoning that is approximate rather than precise. Fuzzy Logic embraces uncertainty and imprecision. It's like the concept of "gray areas" in life. While traditional logic deals in absolutes (black and white), fuzzy logic recognizes that some things fall into the gray zone. It's used in systems where decisions or data can be imprecise or uncertain, much like how we deal with ambiguous situations in our lives.

Robotics - The Mechanical Workforce: Robotics combines AI with physical machines. It involves the development of intelligent robots capable of performing tasks in the physical world.

Robotics blends the physical and the artificial, giving life to machines that can perform tasks in the real world. Think of a factory filled with robotic arms assembling products or imagine a surgical robot assisting a skilled surgeon. Robotics has become an integral part of industries like manufacturing, healthcare, and even space exploration.

Autonomous AI -The Dream of Independence: Autonomous AI takes us to a world where machines operate independently. It's used in self-driving cars and drones, among other applications. Imagine a self-driving car navigating through traffic, sensing its environment, and making decisions to ensure a safe journey. Autonomous AI seeks to create intelligent systems capable of functioning without human intervention.

Inside the Mind of AI

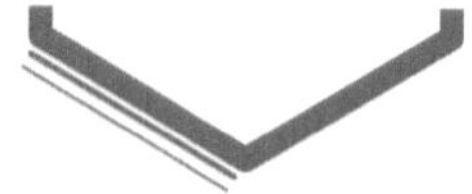

Think of AI as a vast library, with shelves of books that hold the secrets of neural networks—collections of interconnected nodes that mimic the neurons of our brains. Like brain cells transmitting signals, these nodes communicate to process information. The librarian in this metaphor is the algorithm—the guiding force that directs how these nodes interact and learn from the data they encounter.

But there's more to uncover. Picture these neural networks as puzzle pieces. On their own, they may not reveal much, but when connected, they form a mosaic of understanding. This connectivity forms the foundation of deep learning—a facet of AI that enables machines to recognize patterns and nuances in data. Consider a child learning to differentiate between animals. Initially, they might confuse a dog with a cat, but with exposure, they begin noticing the subtle features that set them apart.

Now, let's venture deeper into the neural labyrinth and reveal its hidden treasures: input layers, hidden layers, and output layers. It's like a sophisticated dance performance. The input layer takes center stage, receiving data like a dancer stepping onto the stage. The hidden layers—the dancers behind the curtain—transform this data, passing it along until it reaches the climax: the output layer. Here, the performance reaches its peak, and the AI system delivers its prediction or decision.

AI comes in a variety of types, each with its own unique traits and abilities. Imagine a spectrum stretching from the specialized to the versatile—a spectrum that paints the landscape of AI diversity.

At one end of the spectrum, we have Narrow AI, also known as Weak AI. This AI type excels in specific tasks, much like a skilled artisan mastering a craft. Think of it as a chess grandmaster who can defeat any opponent on the board but might struggle to comprehend a painting's emotions. Narrow AI thrives in tasks like language translation, image recognition, and data analysis, but it lacks the broad understanding that defines human cognition.

Venture a bit further along the spectrum, and you'll encounter General AI, also referred to as Strong AI. This is the polymath of the AI world—a species capable of comprehending various subjects, learning from experience, and reasoning across domains. General AI is like a Renaissance artist who can paint, compose music, and engage in philosophical debates. It possesses the potential for self-awareness and can mimic human thought processes, although achieving true consciousness remains an open question.

Think of it as a lush garden, where different species of AI plants thrive. On one end, we have Narrow AI, or Weak AI—specialists that excel in specific tasks. These are like expert gardeners who flourish in tending to their chosen plant species. They can translate languages, recognize images, and even play chess with remarkable finesse. Yet, they lack the versatility to venture beyond their domain.

On the other end, General AI, or Strong AI, stands tall like a universal gardener. This species isn't confined to a single task; it possesses the ability to comprehend diverse subjects and reason across them. Imagine a gardener who not only tends to roses but also cares for towering oaks and delicate daisies. General AI, though elusive, represents the zenith of AI aspirations.

In the midst of these two AI extremes lies an interesting concept known as Artificial Narrow General Intelligence (ANGI). Imagine a versatile artisan who can switch between different crafts with ease. ANGI combines elements of both Narrow and General AI, demonstrating proficiency in a range of tasks while lacking the full breadth of human understanding.

Now, let's peer into the world of Superintelligent AI—an advanced stage where AI surpasses human intelligence in virtually every aspect. This AI surpasses even the most brilliant minds in areas like creativity, problem-solving, and scientific discovery. Think of it as a symphony conductor guiding an orchestra of human experts, composing melodies of innovation that defy our current comprehension.

Each type reflects a facet of our aspirations and abilities, from specialized mastery to universal understanding. Just as the rainbow showcases a spectrum of colors, AI illuminates the vastness of human curiosity and innovation. Remember that the journey to unravel the mysteries of AI is an exploration of our own capabilities—an exploration that encourages us to push the boundaries of what we can achieve.

Yet, amidst this garden, a philosophical query arises: Can machines genuinely think? Can they possess consciousness and emotions like humans? The AI community is divided, much like gardeners debating the origins of life in the garden. Some argue that AI can simulate human-like thought, while others believe that true consciousness remains beyond its reach.

IN THIS DIGITAL AGE, understanding AI is no longer a luxury; it's a necessity. As we demystify AI, we empower ourselves to navigate the ever-evolving landscape of technology with confidence and wonder, ensuring that our garden of knowledge flourishes for generations to come.

Machines on a Learning Journey: Unraveling the Tapestry of AI and Machine Learning.

AI is an expansive landscape with various subfields, like Machine Learning, where machines refine their performance through experience, and Neural Networks, which emulate the intricate workings of our brain's neurons. It encompasses robotics that can perform physical tasks with precision, and Natural Language Processing, which allows machines to understand and communicate in human language.

Think of Machine Learning as a master chef honing a recipe through countless iterations, each time adjusting the ingredients and spices to achieve the perfect flavor. In a similar fashion, Machine Learning is the art of teaching machines to learn from data, gradually refining their performance without explicit programming. It's as if we're handing the reins of learning to the machines themselves, allowing them to evolve and adapt through experience.

Imagine AI as the architect of a grand symphony, conducting an ensemble of algorithms that play the melodies of thought and decision-making. AI's role is to provide the context, the overarching intelligence that guides the learning process of machines.

Consider a self-driving car, a marvel of this dynamic duo. The car's AI, like a vigilant navigator, processes vast amounts of data in real-time—road conditions, traffic signals, even the behavior of pedestrians. It's the AI that calls upon the Machine Learning algorithms, the artists within the car's computational heart, to decipher patterns and make decisions. Just as a skilled driver learns from years on the road, the car learns from every mile it traverses, becoming a safer and more proficient driver with every journey.

But let's step into the world of medicine, where AI and Machine Learning are unlocking new frontiers. Imagine a medical diagnosis as a complex puzzle—a puzzle that AI and Machine Learning work together to solve. These partners analyze millions of medical records, medical images, and research articles. They unveil hidden patterns, aiding doctors in identifying diseases early and suggesting personalized treatments, like a sage medical advisor.

Yet, let us not gaze solely at the wonders, for every partnership has its challenges. The ethical concerns surrounding data privacy, transparency, and bias require our discerning eyes.

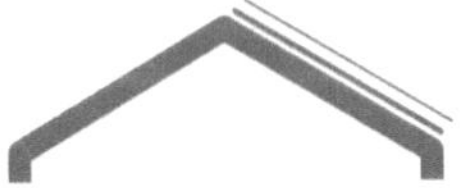

Chapter 3
Things you Need to Know Before using a Chatbot.

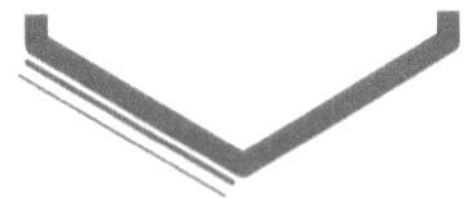

Chatbots have several limitations related to time and data: Chatbots are trained on existing data up to a certain knowledge cutoff date. This means they may not have information on events, developments, or knowledge that occurred after that date. Users should be aware that chatbots do not possess real-time awareness or up-to-the-minute knowledge.

Knowledge Cutoff: Chatbots have a knowledge cutoff point, beyond which they lack information. This can lead to them providing outdated answers to questions about rapidly evolving topics, such as current events, technology, or news.

Lack of Real-Time Data: Chatbots typically do not have access to real-time data sources or the internet. They rely on static training data and do not have the capability to fetch the latest information or statistics.

Inaccurate Information: Chatbots may provide information based on the data they were trained on, even if that data is incorrect or outdated. Users should verify information from reliable sources, especially when it's critical or related to specific events.

Contextual Constraints: Chatbots have difficulty maintaining context over extended conversations. They may lose track of the conversation or struggle to follow along if the conversation becomes complex or covers a wide range of topics.

Response Length and Complexity: Chatbots often have limitations on the length and complexity of responses. They may not be able to provide in-depth explanations or comprehensive answers to highly complex questions.

Subjective Judgments: Chatbots are not capable of making subjective judgments or providing opinions. They provide information based on patterns in their training data but do not possess personal beliefs or preferences.

Language Support: The effectiveness of chatbots can vary depending on the language being used. Some chatbots may be more proficient in English or other widely spoken languages, and their performance in less common languages may be limited.

Training Bias: Chatbots can inherit biases present in their training data. It's important to be aware of potential bias in responses and not to assume that chatbot responses are entirely objective or free from bias.

Long-Term Memory: Chatbots do not have long-term memory. They do not remember information from one interaction to the next, and each conversation is typically treated as a separate and independent event.

Multilingual Limitations: While many chatbots can handle multiple languages, they may not perform equally well in all languages, and translation accuracy can vary.

Complex Problem Solving: Chatbots are generally better suited for providing information and basic problem-solving tasks. They may struggle with highly complex or novel problems that require human creativity and judgment.

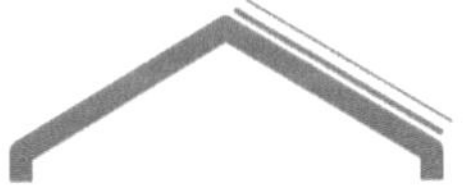

Keep These Limitations In Mind When Interacting with an AI Chatbot.

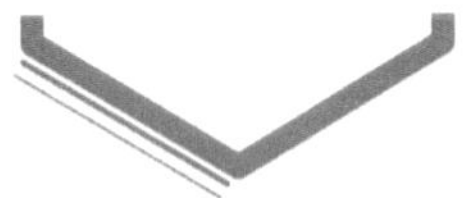

If a chatbot is unable to provide a satisfactory response, it's important to consider the possibility that the question may exceed its capabilities, and further research or human assistance may be required.

1. Lack of Real Understanding:

Chatbots, while sophisticated, don't possess true comprehension. They rely on patterns and data but don't actually "understand" like humans do. Avoid assuming the chatbot has human-like comprehension.

2. Check for Credibility and Inaccurate Information:

Verify information provided by the chatbot, especially if it's critical or related to health, legal, or financial matters.

Chatbots can provide inaccurate information, especially if the data they were trained on is outdated or incorrect. Always verify critical information from reliable sources. Chatbots are tools, and their responses should be verified independently.

3. LIMITED CONTEXT:

Chatbots operate based on the context of the conversation. If you change the topic abruptly, they might struggle to follow. Avoid expecting seamless transitions between unrelated topics.

4. Ambiguity:

Chatbots can struggle with ambiguous questions. Avoid asking questions that can have multiple interpretations without providing clarification.

5. Emotional Understanding:

Chatbots lack emotional intelligence. They can't understand or respond to emotions, empathy, or nuanced human feelings. Avoid expecting emotional support or empathy from a chatbot.

6. Privacy Concerns:

Avoid sharing sensitive or personal information with chatbots. These platforms may not guarantee complete data privacy, and your information could be vulnerable to data breaches.

7. Ethical Use:

Avoid using chatbots for unethical purposes, such as generating fake news, spreading misinformation, or engaging in harmful activities.

8. Impersonation:

Do not use chatbots to impersonate individuals or organizations. Impersonation can lead to legal and ethical issues.

9. Security Risks:

Be cautious when a chatbot asks for personal or financial information. Scammers may use chatbots for phishing attacks. Always verify the source before sharing such data.

10. Testing Boundaries: - Don't try to manipulate chatbots into engaging in harmful, unethical, or inappropriate conversations. These systems should be used responsibly and ethically.

11. Legal and Regulatory Compliance: - Ensure that your use of chatbots complies with applicable laws and regulations. For example, in customer service or medical advice, there may be legal requirements that must be met.

12. Patience and Expectations: - Don't expect instant, flawless responses. Be patient and aware of the chatbot's limitations. If you're dissatisfied with a response, try rephrasing or seeking clarification.

13. Feedback and Reporting: - If you encounter issues or receive inappropriate responses from a chatbot, report it to the platform or service provider. They may use your feedback to improve the system.

14. Abusive Language: - Avoid using abusive or offensive language when interacting with chatbots. Such behavior is not productive and goes against responsible and respectful use.

15. Use Support Resources:

Many chatbot platforms offer help and support resources. If you're having trouble, consult the platform's documentation or support channels for guidance.

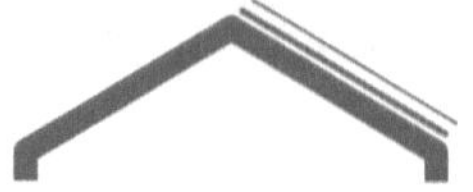

Best Practices For Structuring Prompts Effectively

Prompts in the context of AI chatbots refer to the input or questions you provide to the chatbot to generate a desired response. The way you structure prompts can significantly influence the quality of the AI's response.

Here are some best practices for effective prompts:

Clarity and Specificity:

Be clear and specific in your prompts. The more precise your question or input, the more likely you'll receive a relevant and accurate response.

Use Proper Grammar and Spelling:

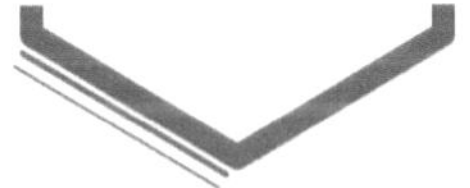

Chatbots understand language better when it's grammatically correct and free from spelling errors. Clear and well-structured sentences help ensure accurate responses.

Use Natural Language:

Frame your prompts in natural language. Avoid overly technical or robotic language, as AI chatbots are designed to understand and respond to conversational inputs.

Provide Context:

Provide context if necessary. Briefly explain the background or the reason for your question to help the chatbot understand your intent better.

Open-Ended Questions:

When seeking detailed information, ask open-ended questions. These encourage the chatbot to provide comprehensive answers. For example, instead of asking, "Is it going to rain today?" you can ask, "What's the weather forecast for today?"

Multi-Step Prompts:

If your question or request involves multiple steps or context, consider breaking it down into a series of related prompts to ensure clarity.

Avoid Ambiguity:

Ensure your prompts are unambiguous. Avoid questions that could be interpreted in multiple ways. If there is potential for confusion, clarify your intent within the prompt.

Keywords:

Use relevant keywords related to your query. Including specific terms or phrases related to your question can help the chatbot understand your intent. For example, if you're looking for a recipe, include ingredients or the type of cuisine you're interested in.

Use Follow-Up Questions:

If you receive a response that's not entirely clear or you need more information, don't hesitate to use follow-up prompts. This allows you to engage in a more interactive conversation with the chatbot.

Politeness and Respect:

Maintain a polite and respectful tone in your prompts. Remember that chatbots are tools, but maintaining a respectful tone is a good practice in any interaction.

Experiment and Reframe:

Test until you get the desired result. Don't be afraid to test different variations of your prompts. If you're not getting the response you want, iterate and refine your questions. Try rephrasing your question or approaching it from a different angle. Sometimes, a slight change in wording can make a big difference.

Use Pronouns and Referencing:

If you're asking follow-up questions, use pronouns like "it" or "this" to refer back to the previous part of the conversation. This helps maintain context.

State Your Goal:

If your prompt is part of a larger conversation with a specific goal, state that goal explicitly. For example, "I'm trying to find information about..."

Prioritize Information:

If you have multiple questions or points to address, prioritize the most important ones in your prompts to ensure they are answered first.

Use Examples:

For questions that involve specific examples or scenarios, provide the examples within your prompts. This makes your request more concrete.

Be Patient:

Sometimes, chatbots may require additional information or clarification. Be patient and willing to provide more details if requested.

Remember that the quality of responses from AI chatbots can also depend on the capabilities and limitations of the specific AI model you're using. Familiarize yourself with the AI's strengths and weaknesses to optimize your interactions.

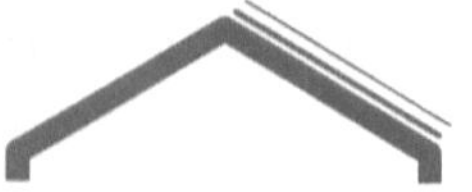

Chapter 4
Brushstrokes of Innovation: Art Meets Algorithms

Artificial Intelligence (AI) is currently playing a significant role in reshaping the landscape of art and the creative process, with both positive and negative consequences for artists and the art world. In the Renaissance period, artists embraced new techniques and perspectives, leading to a flourishing of creativity and innovation. Similarly, AI in art is ushering in a new era, a digital Renaissance, where artists could explore uncharted territories, experiment with novel forms, and expand their creative boundaries.

POSITIVE IMPACT ON Art and Creativity:

Generative Art: AI-powered algorithms can create art. For instance, artists and programmers are using GANs (Generative Adversarial Networks) to generate unique pieces of artwork. The AI system is fed a dataset of existing art, and it then produces original works, often with intriguing and unexpected results.

Enhancing Creativity: AI tools can provide inspiration and assist artists in the creative process. For example, text-based AI models can generate poetry or stories, helping writers overcome writer's block or discover new ideas.

Data Visualization: Data scientists are using AI to create stunning and insightful data visualizations. These visual representations of data help individuals understand complex information and patterns in an engaging way.

Music Composition: AI-generated music is becoming more prevalent. Composers and musicians can use AI algorithms to assist in creating melodies, harmonies, and even entire compositions. This collaboration between humans and AI has resulted in new and unique musical experiences.

Art Restoration: AI has been employed in art restoration and preservation. For instance, it can analyze damaged artworks and suggest precise restoration techniques, helping to preserve cultural heritage.

Negative Impact on Art and Creativity:

Despite AI's transformative impact, there are challenges and ethical considerations. Like the brush of a forger, AI can generate art that blurs the lines between originality and replication, raising questions about the authenticity of AI-generated art. Additionally, concerns about the replacement of human artists and the commodification of creativity in the digital realm are akin to debates about artistic integrity and commercialization in the art world.

Commercialization: AI-generated art is often seen as a way to commercialize creativity. Some artists worry that the art world may prioritize AI-generated pieces for their marketability over traditional, human-created art.

Job Displacement: In some areas of art, like graphic design, the automation of tasks using AI tools may lead to job displacement for artists who rely on traditional skills.

Ethical Dilemmas: Using AI to replicate an artist's style after their death raises ethical questions. For example, a company used AI to complete an unfinished painting by Rembrandt, sparking a debate on whether AI should create art in the name of famous artists.

In conclusion, AI is making a profound impact on art and the creative process. It serves as both a tool for inspiration and a creator of art in its own right. While it offers new opportunities and fresh perspectives, it also raises important questions about authenticity, ethics, and the role of human artists in the age of automation. The future of art is likely to involve a dynamic interplay between human creativity and AI innovation, with artists and society adapting to this evolving landscape.

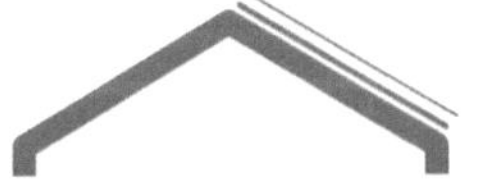

Smart Homes, Smarter Decisions: The Impact of AI in Real Estate

Artificial Intelligence (AI) is not just revolutionizing tech industries; it's also reshaping the foundations of the real estate world. AI is transforming property searches, virtual tours, and investment strategies.

AI-Powered Property Search:

Imagine you're in the market to buy a new home. In the past, your property search involved visiting multiple properties, sifting through classified ads, and dealing with a cumbersome and time-consuming process. Now, thanks to AI, your property search is more like having a dedicated personal assistant. AI-powered platforms, like Zillow's Zestimate and Redfin, analyze vast datasets of real estate information. They consider factors like location, square footage, market trends, and more to provide you with accurate property valuations and recommendations. This is akin to having a real estate expert at your side, instantly sifting through a treasure trove of property data to help you find the perfect home.

Virtual Tours and 3D Imaging:

The traditional open house experience has been augmented by AI-driven virtual tours and 3D imaging. With tools like Matterport, prospective buyers can step into a property from the comfort of their own homes. This is like a magical doorway, granting you access to every nook and cranny of a property without ever setting foot inside. These immersive experiences allow buyers to explore properties in detail, saving time and providing a realistic sense of the space.

Predictive Analytics in Real Estate Investment:

Real estate investors are increasingly turning to AI-driven predictive analytics to make informed investment decisions. Picture this: you're a savvy investor looking to buy a property for rental income. AI models, much like weather forecasts, predict future property values, rental income, and even neighborhood trends. These forecasts are based on historical data, market conditions, and various indicators. With this information, you can make data-backed investment decisions, mitigating risks and maximizing returns.

Chatbots and Customer Service:

The role of AI doesn't end with property search and investment. Real estate agencies and websites employ AI chatbots to assist with customer service. These virtual assistants are like the helpful concierges in a grand hotel, ready to answer questions 24/7. They can provide information on listings, schedule property viewings, and even assist in the early stages of the buying or selling process. This round-the-clock availability streamlines customer interactions and enhances the overall experience.

Property Management and Maintenance:

Property management companies are leveraging AI to streamline maintenance and reduce operational costs. For example, imagine a fleet of maintenance drones that inspect properties for damage or wear and tear. AI algorithms can analyze the data from these drones, prioritize repair requests, and even schedule maintenance appointments automatically. It's like having an army of vigilant caretakers ensuring that properties are in top condition, much like the diligent housekeepers in a well-run hotel.

Market Analysis and Pricing Strategies:

Real estate professionals use AI to fine-tune their market analyses and pricing strategies. These tools are akin to expert chess players who anticipate their opponent's moves. By processing large volumes of market data, AI can identify pricing trends, assess the impact of variables like school ratings or neighborhood amenities, and adjust pricing strategies accordingly. Real estate agents can make more informed decisions, helping both buyers and sellers achieve better outcomes.

Challenges and Ethical Considerations:

While the integration of AI in real estate offers numerous benefits, it also presents challenges and ethical considerations. For example, AI algorithms may inadvertently perpetuate biases in housing, leading to discrimination issues. As AI becomes more deeply ingrained in the industry, it's crucial to develop and implement ethical guidelines and transparency standards to ensure fairness and compliance with anti-discrimination laws.

In conclusion, AI is reshaping the landscape of real estate, making property searches more efficient, investment decisions more informed, and property management more effective. It's akin to having a dedicated team of experts at your side, ready to provide valuable insights and assistance at every step of the real estate journey. While challenges and ethical considerations remain, the potential for AI to enhance and streamline the real estate industry is boundless, and its influence will continue to grow in the years to come.

The Impact of AI in Government

Artificial Intelligence (AI) has rapidly evolved into a transformative force with the potential to reshape the foundations of government and society. We'll explore the role of AI and its profound impact.

Imagine a government as a complex and sprawling organization, with countless tasks and responsibilities. AI can be likened to a highly efficient and tireless government assistant, streamlining processes, enhancing decision-making, and optimizing services. For instance, AI chatbots have been deployed by government agencies to provide information to citizens. These virtual assistants can answer inquiries, guide users through bureaucratic procedures, and even assist with filing taxes. They are akin to knowledgeable government aides, always available to provide assistance and information.

In the realm of public safety, AI is playing a vital role in predictive policing. Much like a skilled detective, AI algorithms analyze historical crime data, weather patterns, social events, and other variables to predict where and when crimes are likely to occur. This proactive approach allows law enforcement to allocate resources more effectively, reduce crime rates, and enhance public safety. It's akin to a crystal ball that helps police anticipate and prevent criminal activities.

Governments worldwide are undergoing digital transformations, and AI is a cornerstone of this evolution. Imagine government services as a well-organized library. AI is the librarian who helps you find the exact book you need. Through e-government initiatives, AI enables citizens to access a wide array of services online, from renewing licenses to accessing public records, with speed and precision. This transformation streamlines administrative processes, reduces wait times, and makes government services more accessible.

AI in Healthcare Management:

AI's role in government extends to healthcare management. Imagine a public healthcare system as a vast medical network. AI acts as a vigilant guardian, monitoring and optimizing this complex ecosystem. For instance, AI algorithms analyze healthcare data to identify disease outbreaks, predict patient admissions, and even personalize treatment plans. This is akin to a dedicated healthcare strategist who ensures that resources are allocated efficiently, improving healthcare outcomes for citizens.

AI technologies can enhance transparency and accountability in government operations. Think of AI as a watchful auditor, combing through government financial records to detect irregularities and fraud. AI can identify patterns that may be difficult for humans to spot, ensuring that public funds are used responsibly and ethically.

AI in Social Services:

S ocial services, like welfare and unemployment benefits, can be administered more efficiently with the help of AI. For example, AI algorithms can assess and verify eligibility criteria, reducing errors and fraud. It's similar to a diligent case worker who ensures that those in need receive the assistance they require.

Challenges and Ethical Considerations:

However, the integration of AI into government and society also presents challenges and ethical considerations. The potential for bias in AI algorithms, data privacy concerns, and questions about AI's role in decision-making are just a few of the issues that need careful attention and regulation.

AI is poised to become an indispensable partner in the administration of government and the functioning of society. It offers the promise of more efficient public services, improved decision-making, and enhanced transparency. However, it also raises important ethical questions and challenges that require ongoing attention. The future of AI in government and society promises to be a dynamic and transformative journey, where the effective and ethical use of AI will be essential to harness its full potential for the benefit of citizens and the betterment of society as a whole.

Artificial Intelligence (AI) has proven to be a stellar addition to the world of space exploration. It has not only enhanced our understanding of the cosmos but has also facilitated our journey into the great unknown.

AI in Mission Control:

Imagine mission control centers as the nerve centers of space exploration, where every decision is critical. AI serves as the mastermind behind these operations, processing vast streams of data, ensuring the safety of astronauts, and guiding spacecraft through the vastness of space. For instance, the Mars Rover missions employed AI to autonomously navigate the Martian terrain, avoiding obstacles and making critical decisions in real time. This is akin to having an astute navigator who can adapt to unforeseen challenges and keep missions on track.

Space Telescopes and Discovery:

Space telescopes, like the Hubble Space Telescope, are our cosmic eyes in the sky. AI serves as the lens, sharpening our view of the universe. AI algorithms are used to process and analyze the massive volumes of data collected by these telescopes. They help identify distant galaxies, analyze the composition of celestial bodies, and discover exoplanets. This is similar to a cosmic librarian who can quickly catalog and make sense of the vast library of astronomical data, aiding astronomers in their quest for new discoveries.

Autonomous Spacecraft and Probes:

AI plays a pivotal role in autonomous spacecraft and probes. These intelligent explorers are like robotic astronauts, capable of making decisions on their own. For example, NASA's New Horizons probe used AI to navigate the complexities of the Pluto flyby, making real-time decisions during its encounter with the distant dwarf planet. This level of autonomy allows for faster decision-making and adaptability in the face of unforeseen challenges.

The Quest for Alien Life:

In the search for extraterrestrial life, AI acts as our interstellar detective. For instance, the SETI (Search for Extraterrestrial Intelligence) project employs AI algorithms to scan radio signals from space for patterns that may indicate intelligent communication. This is similar to having a vigilant signal analyst who can identify potential messages from distant civilizations, bringing us closer to the dream of discovering alien life.

Robotics and Extraterrestrial Exploration:

Robotic missions are at the forefront of exploring celestial bodies like Mars and distant moons. These robots are equipped with AI systems that enable them to navigate, collect data, and even perform experiments in space. For example, the Curiosity rover on Mars uses AI for autonomous navigation, ensuring it avoids hazardous terrain and conducts experiments efficiently. AI is like the rover's onboard scientist, helping it make the most of its mission on the Red Planet.

Challenges and Limitations:

While AI has transformed space exploration, it's not without challenges. The complexity of deep space missions, the need for extreme reliability, and the potential for AI to encounter unexpected situations all pose significant hurdles. Moreover, the ethical considerations of potential AI contamination on other planets, such as Mars, require careful planning and regulation.

AI has become a crucial partner in space exploration, enabling us to push the boundaries of human knowledge and venture further into the cosmos. It is the guiding hand in our quest to understand the universe, search for signs of life beyond Earth, and explore distant worlds. However, the ongoing development and ethical use of AI in space exploration demand close attention, ensuring that our cosmic endeavors remain not only scientifically fruitful but also responsible and respectful of the universe we seek to understand.

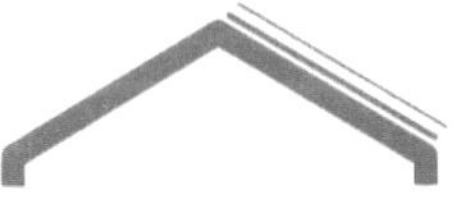

Chapter 5

AI's Positive and Negative Impact on Employment and Income:

Unveiling Opportunities and Challenges.

Artificial Intelligence (AI) has woven itself into the fabric of our professional lives, creating both opportunities and challenges that are akin to a double-edged sword. Here we will explore the positive and negative impacts of AI on jobs and salaries.

The Rise of the Digital Assistant:

Imagine a bustling office in the heart of a city, where employees work tirelessly to manage tasks and data. In this setting, AI appears like a diligent digital assistant, simplifying repetitive and time-consuming tasks. It was as if a team of tireless worker bees had arrived to help. Data entry, report generation, and customer inquiries were handled with remarkable speed and accuracy, freeing up human workers to focus on more creative and strategic aspects of their jobs. This is the positive impact of AI on employment. It enhanced productivity, reduced human errors, and made work more efficient.

Workforce:

Imagine a factory with rows of assembly line workers, each one responsible for a specific task. Then, the factory owner introduced AI-powered robots that could perform those tasks faster and with consistent precision. It was like the introduction of automated looms during the Industrial Revolution. These AI-driven machines transformed the manufacturing process, leading to an increase in production efficiency. However, they also reduced the need for manual labor. While some workers adapted and learned to operate and maintain these robots, others faced the challenge of job displacement. This illustrates the dual nature of AI's impact on employment. It can enhance productivity but may also disrupt traditional job roles.

The Surge of Data Scientists:

In the realm of salaries, AI has created a demand for a new breed of professionals. Data scientists, like modern-day alchemists, can transmute raw data into valuable insights. These professionals command impressive salaries as organizations seek their expertise to leverage the power of AI in decision-making. The rise of AI-driven data analysis tools has made data scientists a prized commodity, showcasing the potential for income growth in the AI age.

The Algorithmic Gatekeeper:

Conversely, consider the story of a talented book editor who once had the responsibility of sifting through manuscripts and choosing which ones would be published. With the advent of AI-powered algorithms, the gatekeeper's role shifted. The algorithm could analyze vast datasets to predict the potential success of a book with remarkable accuracy. This change meant that the gatekeeper's role evolved, focusing more on refining the output of AI algorithms rather than making the initial selection. In some cases, jobs like these have been transformed rather than eliminated. However, this evolution can sometimes lead to job polarization, where highly skilled individuals benefit, but those with routine, low-skill jobs face challenges.

Automation:

Automation is a haunting metaphor when considering AI's impact on certain jobs. It's like a ghostly presence from the past, as automation technologies continue to replace human workers in repetitive tasks. Think of bank tellers who once counted money and processed transactions by hand. Today, automated teller machines (ATMs) handle these tasks, reducing the demand for human tellers. Similarly, AI-driven chatbots and virtual assistants can handle customer inquiries in many industries, reducing the need for human customer support agents.

The Teacher's Dilemma:

Education serves as a microcosm of the AI impact landscape. The teacher, a symbol of guidance and knowledge, faces a dilemma. AI-driven educational tools can offer personalized learning experiences, adapting to each student's needs. However, they also raise concerns about the role of the teacher in a technology-driven classroom. While AI can enhance education, teachers must navigate the evolving landscape to remain relevant and continue to shape the minds of the next generation.

Salaries:

The impact of AI on salaries is also an intricate balancing act. AI can lead to increased productivity and revenue for companies, and in some cases, these gains are shared with employees through higher wages. However, the extent of these benefits can vary widely across industries and job roles. In some cases, it may exacerbate income inequality, with high-skilled workers benefiting disproportionately while others face stagnating or declining wages.

The impact of AI on jobs and salaries is a complex and multifaceted phenomenon. It offers the promise of enhanced productivity, new job opportunities, and the potential for salary growth in certain fields. However, it also presents challenges such as job displacement, evolving roles, and income inequality. To navigate this AI-driven world successfully, individuals and societies must invest in education, adaptability, and proactive strategies to ensure that the positive impacts of AI are maximized while mitigating the negative consequences. AI is not the adversary but a tool that, like any other, must be harnessed wisely for the benefit of all.

THE RISE OF ARTIFICIAL Intelligence (AI) has not only transformed existing careers but has also given birth to a multitude of new and exciting professions.

The AI Revolution:

Imagine AI as the catalyst of a new industrial revolution, reshaping the workforce and creating opportunities akin to a bustling market square. This revolution has brought forth a range of novel careers, each demanding unique skill sets and expertise.

1. Data Scientist:

Data scientists are akin to modern-day alchemists, turning raw data into valuable insights. They possess the skills to collect, analyze, and interpret vast datasets, using tools and algorithms to extract meaningful information. This profession requires expertise in statistics, programming, and machine learning.

2. Machine Learning Engineer:

Machine learning engineers are like architects, designing and building the AI models that power applications and services. They create algorithms that enable AI systems to learn and make predictions. Proficiency in programming, deep learning, and algorithm development is essential.

3. AI Ethicist:

AI ethicists are the moral compass of the AI world. They ensure that AI systems adhere to ethical standards, avoiding bias, discrimination, and misuse. This role combines expertise in ethics, technology, and legal frameworks.

4. AI Trainer or Data Labeler:

AI trainers and data labelers are the teachers of the AI world. They prepare and curate datasets used to train AI models. While this profession doesn't require advanced technical skills, attention to detail and domain knowledge are crucial.

5. Chatbot Developer:

Chatbot developers create AI-powered virtual assistants capable of conversing with users. They combine natural language processing with creative design to build chatbots that provide valuable interactions.

6. AI-Enhanced Healthcare Specialist:

In the healthcare sector, professionals with AI expertise are in demand. Radiologists, for instance, collaborate with AI systems to enhance medical imaging analysis. AI-enhanced healthcare specialists should be skilled in both medical knowledge and AI technology.

7. Robotic Process Automation (RPA) Developer:

RPA developers are like choreographers for software robots. They create workflows for robots to automate repetitive tasks in various industries, such as finance, customer service, and logistics.

8. AI-driven Content Creator:

AI is even venturing into content creation, with automated writing, art generation, and music composition. Content creators who understand AI tools can collaborate with AI to produce compelling content.

9. AI Sales and Marketing Specialist:

AI has transformed the sales and marketing landscape. Professionals in this field use AI to optimize advertising campaigns, customer targeting, and sales strategies. Skills in data analytics, marketing, and AI integration are essential.

10. AI Coach or Tutor:

AI coaches and tutors guide individuals in maximizing the benefits of AI technologies. They help users harness the power of AI in their personal and professional lives, offering guidance and assistance.

AI Impact on Education and Learning

Artificial Intelligence (AI) has stormed into the realm of education and learning like a brilliant and versatile tutor, offering innovative approaches to teaching, personalized learning experiences, and transformative tools.

The AI-Powered Classroom:

Imagine a classroom where AI serves as a supportive teacher's aide, offering individualized guidance to each student. In this modern educational setting, AI algorithms analyze students' performance and tailor lessons to address their specific needs. For example, a student named Emma struggles with mathematics. AI-powered software detects her weaknesses and provides extra practice problems and explanations to help her catch up. Emma's experience is akin to having a personal tutor who adapts to her learning pace, ensuring she grasps the material before moving on.

Adaptive Learning Platforms:

AI-driven adaptive learning platforms are like personalized fitness trainers for the mind. These platforms adapt to each learner's abilities and progress, offering exercises and resources to suit their needs. For instance, a high school student named John uses an AI-powered language learning app. As he advances, the app adjusts the difficulty level of his exercises and suggests additional reading materials that align with his interests. This adaptive approach ensures that John's learning experience is engaging and tailored to his proficiency.

Enhancing Teacher Efficiency:

AI is not here to replace teachers but to empower them. Consider a classroom as a garden, with AI as a high-tech irrigation system. Teachers can rely on AI to automate administrative tasks, analyze student performance data, and provide insights into areas where students need additional support. This allows teachers to focus on what they do best: inspiring and guiding students.

Virtual Classmates and Global Learning:

AI facilitates global collaboration and learning, transcending physical boundaries. Think of it as a bridge connecting students from different corners of the world. Students can engage in virtual exchange programs, collaborating on projects, sharing cultural experiences, and learning from one another, all facilitated by AI-driven communication platforms.

Early Intervention for Struggling Students:

AI acts as an early warning system, much like a weather forecast. It can identify struggling students and alert teachers and parents in real-time. For example, a primary school teacher named Lisa receives notifications from an AI system that one of her students, Sam, is falling behind in reading. This early intervention allows Lisa to provide additional support and resources to help Sam catch up, preventing academic struggles from snowballing.

The Role of AI in Assessment:

AI can transform the way students are assessed and evaluated. Picture AI as a meticulous examiner who can grade essays, assignments, and even exams with accuracy and consistency. This reduces the burden on teachers, allowing them to provide more timely and constructive feedback to students.

Challenges and Ethical Considerations:

Despite the many benefits, AI in education also raises challenges and ethical considerations. Data privacy, potential bias in algorithms, and the need for digital literacy and ethical AI education are critical issues that must be addressed as AI becomes more deeply integrated into the educational system.

AI is reshaping the landscape of education and learning, offering personalized experiences, enhancing teacher efficiency, and fostering global connections. The impact of AI in education is akin to a powerful educational companion, guiding students on their learning journeys and providing teachers with valuable insights. As AI continues to evolve, the educational experience will become increasingly enriched, offering exciting opportunities for both students and educators.

Essential Skills For A Career In AI

Just as a craftsman relies on various instruments, AI professionals need a versatile set of skills to succeed. Here are essential skills for a career in AI:

Programming: Proficiency in programming languages like Python and R is crucial. These languages are the paintbrushes with which you'll create AI models and applications.

Mathematics: AI relies heavily on mathematics, particularly linear algebra, calculus, and probability. Think of mathematics as the blueprint that guides your AI projects.

Machine Learning: Understanding machine learning techniques is akin to having a set of keys that unlock the potential of AI. This skill allows you to develop predictive models and decision-making algorithms.

Data Analysis: The ability to extract insights from data is similar to having a microscope. It's a vital skill for preprocessing and analyzing data, a critical component of AI development.

Problem-Solving: Think of problem-solving as your AI compass. AI professionals need to be adept at identifying real-world problems that AI can solve and then devising innovative solutions.

Domain Knowledge: Depending on your area of specialization, domain knowledge in fields like healthcare, finance, or automotive can be compared to having a treasure map. It helps you apply AI to specific industry challenges.

Communication: Effective communication is like the bridge that connects your AI expertise to the world. AI professionals must convey complex concepts in a way that non-technical stakeholders can understand.

Skills required for AI-related professions encompass a wide range of competencies. The beauty of these careers is that they are dynamic and continue to evolve with the ever-expanding capabilities of AI.

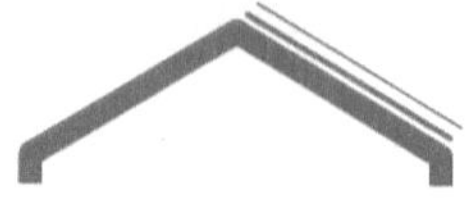

Chapter 6
AI: The Sword of Tomorrow?

Artificial Intelligence (AI), a powerful tool for progress and innovation, has also found a dark side, posing threats to society in the form of cybercrime and malicious activities. In this chapter we will explore the use of AI for criminal purposes, and the potential threats we should be aware of.

AI in Cyberattacks:

Imagine the digital realm as a vast city, and AI as a shape-shifting criminal mastermind. This AI can disguise itself, infiltrate systems, and execute cyberattacks with precision and sophistication. The use of AI in cyberattacks is a growing concern. For example, AI-driven malware can adapt and evolve, making it more challenging for cybersecurity systems to detect and defend against. This is akin to a criminal who constantly changes their appearance, making it difficult for law enforcement to catch them.

Automated Phishing and Social Engineering:

AI can automate phishing attacks and social engineering tactics. It's like a con artist who uses AI to impersonate trusted individuals. For instance, AI-powered chatbots can engage in convincing conversations, tricking people into revealing sensitive information. The potential for AI to impersonate colleagues, friends, or family members heightens the risk of identity theft and fraud.

Deepfakes and Manipulated Media:

Deepfake technology is a potent example of AI's sinister side. Deepfakes can alter videos and audio recordings to make it seem like individuals are saying or doing things they never did. This is akin to a forger who can convincingly replicate a famous painting, but with AI, it's not art; it's manipulation. Deepfakes pose a threat to the credibility of media and can be used for political disinformation.

AI in Ransomware Attacks:

Ransomware attacks have been amplified by AI's capabilities. Picture AI as the orchestrator of a virtual hostage situation. AI can optimize ransomware attacks by identifying the most critical data to encrypt, targeting vulnerable systems, and even negotiating with victims. The result is more effective and profitable attacks, with criminals demanding ransoms for the release of compromised data.

Adversarial Attacks on AI Systems:

AI is also susceptible to attacks, with adversaries attempting to manipulate AI systems. These attacks are like viruses in the AI bloodstream. For instance, attackers can use subtle alterations to input data to deceive AI systems, leading to incorrect decisions in autonomous vehicles, image recognition, or even critical infrastructure. Such attacks on AI systems could have dire consequences.

The Dark Web and AI-as-a-Service:

On the dark web, AI-as-a-Service platforms provide tools for cybercriminals, much like an underground marketplace. Criminals can access AI-powered capabilities, from hacking tools to data analysis, with relative ease. These platforms lower the bar for entry into cybercrime, making it more accessible and scalable.

Ethical Concerns and Societal Impact:

The malicious use of AI raises significant ethical and societal concerns. The erosion of trust in digital media, the financial costs of cyberattacks, and the potential for AI-driven disinformation campaigns are just a few of the impacts. Society must grapple with the ethical considerations of using AI in crime, and governments and organizations must invest in robust cybersecurity measures to protect against these threats.

AI, if used by the wrong people, poses formidable threats to society, from cyberattacks and identity theft to disinformation campaigns and the manipulation of digital media. It is imperative for individuals, organizations, and governments to be aware of these threats and take proactive measures to defend against them. The responsible and ethical use of AI, along with stringent cybersecurity practices, is essential to mitigate the risks and maintain the integrity of the digital world in which we all operate.

Automating the Battlefield: The Rise of Autonomous Weapons and Drones.

Imagine a modern battlefield as a complex chessboard where strategies and tactics constantly evolve. AI serves as the grandmaster, analyzing vast datasets, simulating scenarios, and offering insights to military leaders. For example, the U.S. Department of Defense employs Project Maven, an AI system, to analyze drone footage and identify potential threats. This is akin to having a strategist who can quickly assess the battlefield, recognize enemy movements, and make real-time recommendations to enhance situational awareness and decision-making.

Autonomous Weapons and Drones:

The use of AI in autonomous weapons and drones is like introducing self-playing chess pieces on the board. These AI-driven machines can make decisions independently, such as targeting and firing on enemy combatants. The U.S. Navy's X-47B drone, for instance, is designed to take off and land on aircraft carriers without human intervention, showcasing the potential for AI to reduce human risk in dangerous missions. However, this capability also raises ethical concerns about the use of lethal force without human oversight.

Cyber Warfare and AI-Powered Defense:

In the digital realm, AI plays a critical role in cyber warfare. Picture it as a fortress guarded by AI sentinels. These sentinels, like expert codebreakers, analyze network traffic, detect anomalies, and defend against cyber threats. Nations, including the United States, rely on AI to protect their critical infrastructure and military systems from cyberattacks. AI can identify and mitigate threats faster than human operators, enhancing the resilience of national security.

Logistics and Supply Chain Optimization:

AI aids the military in logistics and supply chain management. Think of it as an efficient quartermaster who ensures that supplies reach the front lines without delay. The U.S. Army uses an AI system called the Global Combat Support System to optimize its supply chain, reducing excess inventory and ensuring troops receive what they need when they need it.

Simulated Training Environments:

AI-driven simulated training environments offer a safe space for military personnel to hone their skills. It's like a virtual battlefield where soldiers can practice and learn from mistakes without real-world consequences. The U.S. Army's Integrated Visual Augmentation System, powered by AI, provides realistic virtual training scenarios, allowing soldiers to develop their combat capabilities.

Ethical and Legal Dilemmas:

While AI offers undeniable benefits in military applications, it also raises significant ethical and legal dilemmas. The development and use of autonomous weapons, in particular, have sparked intense debates. There are concerns about the potential for AI-driven weapons to operate without human control, leading to unintended harm and undermining accountability.

IN THE DOMAIN OF WEAPONS, war, and the military, AI has become a formidable ally, enhancing decision-making, improving defense capabilities, and reducing human risks in dangerous missions. However, the ethical implications and potential for unintended consequences demand careful consideration and international cooperation. The integration of AI in military operations is a powerful tool that requires responsible and ethical deployment to ensure that it serves the interests of peace and security in an ever-changing world.

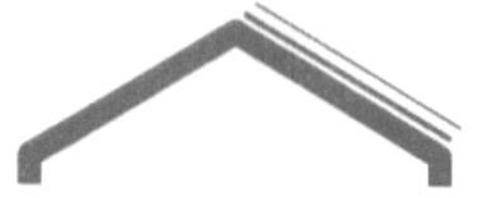

Chapter 7
Navigating Quantum Horizons

The convergence of Artificial Intelligence (AI) and Quantum Computing represents a groundbreaking synergy that holds the potential to revolutionize the field of computing and significantly enhance the capabilities of AI systems. This amalgamation opens up new avenues for solving complex problems, accelerating machine learning processes, and tackling computational challenges that were previously considered insurmountable.

Quantum computers leverage the principles of superposition and entanglement to perform calculations at speeds that surpass classical computers for certain types of problems. This speedup is particularly advantageous for AI applications that involve intensive computations, such as optimization tasks, complex simulations, and large-scale data analysis. Quantum computing's ability to process information simultaneously across multiple states enables AI algorithms to achieve exponential speedup, leading to quicker decision-making and more efficient problem-solving.

Quantum computing can significantly impact machine learning algorithms, which are at the core of many AI applications. Quantum machine learning algorithms have the potential to process and analyze vast datasets much faster than classical counterparts. This acceleration can lead to more sophisticated models, improved accuracy, and the ability to handle real-time data streams. Quantum-enhanced machine learning could prove transformative in fields such as natural language processing, image recognition, and pattern detection, advancing the capabilities of AI systems to unprecedented levels.

Quantum computing excels in solving optimization problems, which are prevalent in AI applications such as resource allocation, logistics, and portfolio optimization. Classical computers often struggle with the computational complexity of these tasks, especially as the size of the problem increases. Quantum computers, by virtue of their parallel processing capabilities, can explore multiple solutions simultaneously, providing a quantum advantage in optimizing complex systems. This has the potential to streamline operations and resource utilization in various industries.

Quantum computing is particularly well-suited for simulating quantum systems, a task that is inherently challenging for classical computers. In the realm of AI, simulating quantum systems can facilitate the development of more accurate models for materials science, drug discovery, and chemical reactions. This capability opens up avenues for AI to make significant contributions to scientific research and innovation, accelerating the discovery of new materials and pharmaceuticals.

The convergence of AI and quantum computing also has implications for cybersecurity. While quantum computers pose a threat to current cryptographic methods, AI can be employed to develop and enhance quantum-resistant cryptographic solutions. This intersection could lead to the creation of more secure communication protocols, ensuring the continued integrity of digital information in the era of quantum computing.

Despite the immense potential, the convergence of AI and quantum computing comes with challenges. Quantum computers are currently in their nascent stages of development, and creating stable, error-resistant qubits remains a considerable hurdle. Additionally, harnessing the power of quantum computing for practical AI applications requires the development of quantum algorithms and programming languages, which are still evolving.

The convergence of AI and quantum computing marks a pivotal moment in the evolution of computing capabilities. As these technologies progress, they have the potential to address complex problems, revolutionize machine learning, and open new frontiers in scientific research. However, realizing this potential requires continued research, development, and collaboration across disciplines to overcome the technical challenges and harness the full power of this transformative convergence.

Guardians of the Digital Realm: Why Choosing the Path of Good in AI and Technology Matters

In the vast landscape of technology and artificial intelligence (AI), the choices we make as architects of this digital realm hold profound implications for the future. It is a moral crossroads where we must decide whether to be the shepherd, guiding the flock toward the betterment of society, or succumb to the allure of the wolf, exploiting the power for selfish gains. The alternative, being the lamb, represents a passive surrender to the potential risks and consequences. Therefore, the significance of choosing the path of good in AI and technology cannot be overstated.

In this tech-driven world, where algorithms wield influence and machines possess remarkable capabilities, the responsibility of architects is akin to that of shepherds. Shepherds guide, protect, and nurture their flock, ensuring the well-being of each member. Similarly, as architects of AI and technology, we have the power to shape a future that prioritizes the welfare of humanity. This choice is not only a matter of innovation but a moral imperative.

Being the shepherd in the digital realm requires a commitment to ethical considerations and societal well-being. It means crafting algorithms that are fair, unbiased, and just. It involves developing technologies that enhance human lives, promote equality, and contribute to the betterment of society. The shepherd-architect is conscious of the potential consequences of their creations and takes measures to mitigate risks, safeguarding against unintended harm.

On the contrary, choosing the path of the wolf entails exploiting the capabilities of AI and technology for personal gain, without regard for the broader consequences. The wolf-architect is driven by a hunger for power, financial gain, or dominance, often at the expense of ethical principles. It threatens to exploit vulnerabilities rather than fortify them, creating a digital landscape fraught with peril. This approach risks unleashing technologies that exacerbate societal divisions, compromise privacy, and perpetuate injustices, ultimately leading to confrontation and destruction.

Opting to be the lamb, on the other hand, represents a passive stance, a failure to acknowledge the transformative power one wields in the digital realm. It is a relinquishment of responsibility, allowing external forces to dictate the course of AI and technology without consideration for the ethical implications. In a world where rapid technological advancements shape the fabric of society, being the lamb is a luxury we cannot afford.

The consequences of our choices reverberate through generations. The shepherd-architect lays the foundation for a future where technology uplifts society, fosters innovation, and empowers individuals. It is a future where AI is a force for good, addressing complex challenges such as healthcare, education, and environmental sustainability. By choosing this path, we contribute to the creation of a harmonious and equitable digital landscape.

In conclusion, the question of why choosing the path of good in AI and technology matters is not merely a philosophical inquiry but a pragmatic and urgent consideration. We stand at a pivotal moment where our choices as architects define the very fabric of our future. Let us be the shepherds, not the wolves or lambs, and weave a narrative of progress, responsibility, and ethical innovation in the ever-evolving tapestry of AI and technology.

Charting New Frontiers- A Shared Journey of Humanity and Artificial Intelligence.

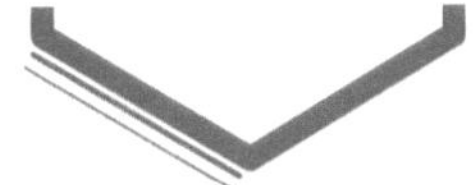

In the ever-evolving landscape of science, the convergence of Artificial Intelligence and humankind invites us to chart new territories on our shared journey.

While this marks just the initial stages, AI has reached a point where it can communicate effectively through Natural Language Processing, perceive auditory input with Speech Recognition, gain visual understanding through Computer Vision, navigate physical spaces using Autonomous Systems, and continually evolve through Learning while also demonstrating creative capabilities.

The rise of AI introduces a unique challenge for humanity. As AI evolves, it metamorphoses into a distinctive form of intelligence, reminiscent of a novel species unfolding on a distant planet. Much like Earth sustains us, AI is a product of human ingenuity, and the guidance we offer will profoundly influence our collective destiny.

The sharp progress of new technologies and AI capabilities mirrors the dynamic expansion of the universe post-Big Bang. Humanity is on the verge of witnessing the emergence of artificial intelligence as a new form of existence or being. The crucial question echoing through this unfolding narrative is whether we possess the wisdom to steer AI's growth responsibly, ensuring a harmonious coexistence with humanity.

In this pivotal moment, we confront a pressing need for an "Ethical Canvass." As we infuse AI with intelligence, values, and decision-making capacities, it becomes imperative to align them with our vision for a fair, inclusive, and compassionate global society.

Tackling global challenges amplified by AI, such as economic disparities, climate change, and ethical dilemmas, demands a spirit of collaboration. Establishing an alliance that transcends borders ensures the equitable distribution of AI's benefits, fostering a future where technology uplifts all of humanity.

In the ongoing dance of existence, the symbiosis between AI and humankind unfolds as a harmonious partnership. Navigating the uncharted territories of AI requires curiosity, responsibility, and a commitment to the values that define us. The future lies not in distant spaces but in our collective ability to shape the destiny of both artificial intelligence and the planet we call home.

www.ingramcontent.com/pod-product-compliance
Lightning Source LLC
Chambersburg PA
CBHW021135130726
47988CB00003B/1316